SAILING TOO FAR

SAILING TOO FAR

Poems by Milton Kessler

HARPER & ROW, PUBLISHERS
New York, Evanston, San Francisco, London

I wish to thank the editors of the following magazines for being the first to publish some of the poems in this book: *Brown's Window, Chelsea, Choice, Epoch, Jam To-Day, The Mysterious Barricades, The Nation, Nine Queen Bees, Prism International, Transatlantic Review.*

And I am grateful to Yaddo and to the Research Foundation of the State University of New York. Their fellowships helped me find privacy and time.

M.K.

FIRST EDITION

Designed by C. Linda Dingler

Library of Congress Cataloging in Publication Data

Kessler, Milton.
    Sailing too far; poems.
    I. Title.
PS3561.E7S2   1974   811'.5'4   73-4098
ISBN 0-06-012354-0
ISBN 0-06-012353-2 (pbk.)

CONTENTS

I

II

III

IV

V

VI

For Arthur and Elizabeth

I

Flight Marker I

Myrtle, Woodbine, Appletrees, Trillium,
here they are. The strength of your arm
stalls at the open gate of the stars.

Feel everything, trust everything!

Venus calls from her dream of earth.
I dream her perfect sleeping oriental face,
her certainty of sexual grace. No storm
flaws her mating with that vast wisdom of the moon.

Feel everything, know everything!

That fragile hope of my uncovered skull
smothers with empty words of bliss. . . .
I am small in this bright cataract of pine.
I stand on the smallest stone.
I am a standing prairie dog
praying for my song.

Lost Song

When the wind in the mosaic pool
shimmered the pebbles as bells
I walked on the blades of shells
and pruned the prickly roses.

When the circlets of ruby beads
braided my fingers with wine
I knelt at the knees of the wind
shadowed in sand as a vine.

In the eye of the wind was a woman
white as a dream of oblivion
crooked at the knees of her son
touching his feet with her hair.

A Boy

Out there a boy
is watering roses.
He holds a long, twisting black hose.
The bushes are frightened.
The flowers
enduring
shiver his noisy coaxing.
It's all right
though, they say,
reassuring.
We know him.
He is gentle,
and, besides,
his long, red shirt, flapping,
entertains us.

The Voice of the Soldier

The voice of the soldier speaks and says:
"I'm lucky, I'm always lucky.
It is lighter than danger that I carry—
My great pack lofts with gold air,
I'm going on with stars, white roses,
Songs of sparkled pinecones homeward.
It is laughter so, it is dancing,
There are maidens warm in salty gardens.
Now, somewhere, as if I were really holy,
I know that my savior is lonely."

Tree

Something
is nibbling
high up
in that alder.

Is it the sun
tasting
the cool nip
of the tree?

Summer's End

The screen says "rain," says "rain,"
silver on the red grasses. Recoiled, aroused,
the bay water unbroken and cold,
I stink with pain.
Don't touch me! All right, I'll touch you.
Chair is, wall is, spider is,
sucks out the last fly.
So? So?
I must do something soon, make arrangements,
leave this floor and window.
My heart is old, my face is wet,
my leg is hemorrhaging under the blanket.
Self-pity is awful.

I've been hurt, I mean really.
I hurt myself, not in tranquility,
lullay, lullay, like a child,
you jerk, you jerk, going the wrong way.

How strange, strange, the rain rises,
leaning, drifting over the brown roofs and porches,
cooling, soothing the punished faces, O healing,
my legs, my body, clench upward for its bliss.

There at the far eave of my heartbreak,
slowly, reverently, the drops ascend like
seeds of stillborn children, silver cells like
bells of children, a surf of children paralyzed,
unreleased and hanging.
Vines, trees, pathways, all things in all declensions,
gather inward, gather under.

O sweetness!

I'm here, I'm here, beneath this bombed soil,
one wheel screaming in a dark wind,
my blood weeping silver children
from my side.
O torture, O wheel of torture!

Stranger woman, I put my arms about your coffin,
your body cringes with rage and disappointment.
What's wrong, dream, what's happening?
My arteries burst in the earth!
The trees explode with my blood!

The question:
Mommy, I found the most beautiful shell.
I was lying in it. Where is it now?

Answer:
When you have a child
I hope you suffer as much as I do.

Time flowers, flounders.
The ferryman falls away,
his last cry so orange with death.
Timbers dirge in the red wind—
Your stars break down.

I take you, I take you.

On the failing shore, little huddles of people,
black fallen fruit, weddings everywhere. . . .

I take you, I take you.
I like you so much. Goodbye! Goodbye!
Take care, everybody. Don't be too lonely. . . .

Flight Marker II

Over a bridge that cannot stand it any more,
past the dead farms that hold their aching trees,
I'm drowning or something—I'm so excited—
the limbs have flown from my body—all washed away.

The wind has given me its child to hold—
riding on my shoulders with its ,stars.

II

A Bombardier's Landscape

My wife in a dark room, weeping,
my son's nightlamp, a *Yahrzeit* candle,
Manhattan, New York, the Hudson River,
the unhealed grave on Staten Island,
all dwindle to abstraction,
to ambiguities of wind and shade,
objective, inorganic,
a bombardier's landscape.

These perspectives tranquilize.
The plane sways like my cradle.
If it exploded this second,
traveler, what would it matter.

Called Home

Tremors, bleeding windows, cloud,
steel doors wailing Woodlawn north—
Just words, a valve shut down, burst,
maimed at last. Called home. . . .
O nothing, nine years, the park is gone.

Disinfectant suffocates the stairs.
C-44, their fourth-floor walk-up door
knows my old key.
Gray walls now, a breath of dead cigars,
Van Gogh's quailing postman glares—
I freeze. I chain the door.
There on my turquoise, pre-war sofa bed
                    How many times!
the ashes of my broken mother's hair.

Enough

Sun on my face
will not be enough.
A drive to the mountains
what would it gain.
This morning I found,
while lovers turned
and I dug for my life
for my grandfather's face;
I found in my fist
with the cellar's decay,
shriveled, rank,
in a deathclamp of tin,
the birthcord, rotted,
of my lonely son.
And then for my face
a furred mouth came.

Constellations

Tateh, Tateh, Tateh,
for you, for you, for you.
My mother wailed, I ran.
My tongue was iodine.
Four walls of martyrdom
were clenching all at once.
Her thousand nipples bled.
Four flights of faces down
I dug beneath the stairs.
Within my truant's grave
I found my father home.
His age was shaved away.
An anguish held his side.
Four hands were not enough
to save him from my love.
I woke, I woke again. . . .
O mamma, mamma, why?
The way she wept in bed.
A thousand times a day
your father washed his hands.
The water ran and ran.
There was that fire once;
the ladder came so close.
We died there on the sill.
I went to work for you.

For you, for you, for you!
O tree of Chanukah,
I can't dance on like this,
for you, for you, for you.
O window, curtain, flower,
the clock, the lamp, the door,
the eye, the nail, the frame:
be lifeless life, be lonely.

Davey

Grandmother Celia, save my David!
Lost, lost, my guns are gone.
Backward he falls through the empty bells—
O well, well . . . Chill at the pond.
Hunting and harvest, seizure, numb,
The maimed ducks drift from grass to weed,
Two blackbirds vanish in the gopher wood,
Sophie, Lou, palms of my childhood.
O Paula, daughter, your ranting father
Needs the mothering, baby, Davey.

Ones

O tolling grasses high
O tassels
O bells
O bells of trees
O bells within that room
Oh never opened
Ones . . .

The Quiet

We try to kiss
goodbye again.
The street is quiet
where I play.

These braces laugh
whenever I know.
Tonight I sleep
in my mother's room.

He bends that face—
my stomach breaks.
I do my work.
My bed is dry.

See my new things
in my attic box:
a telescope,
this book of birds.

When summer stays
I'll have to swim.
O my good father
won't sing anymore.

The Passing Bell

I'll go now
nuzzling
my infant son.
How he warms
against me
in the harbor shower,
how his heart
kicks bravely
the passing bell.
My own ribs
shiver—
this evening rain.
Danny Danny,
the friends are mine.
They cringe with laughter
my mind's away. . . .
The sand is loam,
the harbor mild,
the old scows dirge,
the dawn-wind comes.
Ebb tide:
gull faces
squall
in the rocks.

The Person

It would come like a pond of autumn grass,
older than his whole life would be.

It was his own pure body, ring upon ring
of history, circling his dreaming face.

It was no shame. The punishments of love
were his relief, the room so cold and warm.

His legs now longer than that bed
were strong enough to win each morning's race
into the safety of the school.

Here in my late, dry bed,
I'd take his place.

The Walk Back

That Wednesday
he fled school early.
Gay, free,
the maples charred their sky.

The pain was a baldness,
a gas rain.
Five teeth extracted,
he was wet.

He walked back, shameful,
to their shrunken house,
his shirt trembling,
the sink red.

He held his mouth
against that slaughtered mouth,
two rabid dogs
dismembering his face.

After work love came
to make him warm.
About his neck she wracked
her drowning arms.

O mother, mamma,
how can I eat this?
My teeth are in my grave,
my promise broken.

III

Letter

So they too lecture us on how to live and feel.
Well, they're right, I guess.
My sickness, this halting monolith
of sullen dust I scrape and shave; today,
this face, these stalled eyes,
a mother could not make them weep.
The world passes a doomed face.

It is quite different here this time,
and not surprising, after everything.
Blind, angry, haunted, my windows call
and drench me in my chair; the air is dead
and deep, the breath of my own blessing falls.
These friendships die of love. Fired, we move again,
we move again, again. . . .

O now, there, about us, silent, innocent,
in their own sweet dreams I pray for them,
the leaves, our broken days, descend and gather.
O I'm tired, wife, my mind is late October in the ditch.
Forgive me, I will not call. Live, live,
while I'm away, and David, Paula, fair Daniel,
my father Arthur, my mother Elizabeth, take care;

and you, wife, you are a good woman,
you have nothing to be ashamed of, do you hear,
nothing to be ashamed of, no matter what I've said.

I Am No One Else

Swimming, sunning, my children, my wife,
the sea comes over them, returns them;
it is so far from here it happens.
Who are they? What do I know of them,
my heart of life? There, they laugh, play,
tear each other, return to supper, drowsy with sun.
Where am I, from her cool, lonely bed so far?
Here, I walk, I dream of someone else.
We turn, tremble, with fantasy and cold.
My body is tired, this barn heavy with hay.
I am no one else.
I weep. Only the dark can see my fear.
O help them! A lifetime empties in a breath.
No more, these long long summer nights away.

Surprise

In their cradled Eden at the oceanside
my parents drowse away long mornings.
My father is still honest in his chair.
My mother walks the oceanside
and dreams of my lost summer days away.

It is dawn. I go in. Surprise!
Their small, salvaged bodies,
the sweet hair tucked in,
they both face the same way.
Thank you, thank you, I want to say.
At thirty-five my world is as it stays.

The Willow Songs

This girl, whose hair I dream,
walks like a willow in an endless dawn.
There is no harm in her. She is innocence adrift.
There is no school for her, no work at all.
We call her tragedy. The time loves nothing better.
Lord, let her move among thy searing highways
without shame or grief. Let no gold rapist
soil her sorrow. Her name is dreams,
my neighbor's truant daughter.

I met my mother
at the station.
Everywhere
were sabbath faces.
Golden children
clapped the Hora,
fern and ivy
breathing *Mazel.*
There we danced
and danced again,
whirling willows
in the rain.
Thunder knelt
and drove me back:
"The Sabbath Queen,
the Sabbath Bride."

Where have I come
unknown to me before?
The stone door widens.
The stars move close.

My house is better,
wondrous and mild.
My children dance
for the joy of it.

To rise! To rise!
To sing all day.
Home in the willows.
Home in the rain.

Give me now
my woman to love.
My first woman,
my homely wife.

IV

American Voices: *Late Twentieth Century*

I'm happy. What I do now is my own business.
The old couple, brother and sister, crowd
beside me, as if I were their own black son.
We're frightened.
I look too long at her rose bronze face,
her ivory blouse,
and turn away with pleasant shame.
She is a beautiful color.
And as I show her the white cloud cover over
the frozen great lake, she leans against me.
We help each other. It is our first flight together.
Clouds above us, clouds under us,
we tell our stories. She is from Georgia,
a southern lady, a spinster.
We share the black coffee and the long wait
and change in Chicago, a terrible city,
so many awful homes. My face feels better.
My lover, we are perfect strangers.
It's springtime there you know, she to a
funeral in Los Angeles, I to San Diego
to read old poems.
Clouds above us, clouds beneath us.
O dark mother I confess; yes, I have dreamt
bad subway dreams about your sisters' breasts—
or were they always bad?

I'm happy. What I do now is my own business.
It's been nice. The happy mourners, brothers! sisters!
we come down. They take each other's arm and frown and
go.
They proudly say "goodbye."

The Rant of the Ordinary Life

If only the heavy pain I say to you
were less real than our bodies that feel joy.
I see your howling face
articulate with suicide
tear from my mind
with one last lash of pride
that white terrified horse,
"You're not a man!"
He hears! He who had heard
with his thrilled face the click
of new bone within her cool womb,
he hears and wakes into the ordinary life.

They live a daily life:
all rage fused to one sweet flowering tree
that slowly sails on their stone boat
going down to glory.

Russian Joke

One day I laughed all day, noticing the hump
on my back or the lump. My shoulders fell more
in the photograph than before, and then that
sad late pregnancy in front. . . .
It's all become a joke. I should have known.
My family all dies soon of heart stones.

A Dream of Weeping

The bus was empty when he took his seat
The heater rubbed its solace through his flesh
Upon his neck the winter sun was sweet
He hugged his briefcase to his breast and wept—
O shame shame! No father barked. No bully
   called his name.

Tears were smothering his face with blood, as if
An ancient wound had hemorrhaged in his head—
The driver whirled. "Leave me alone," she cries.
A horse came strangling in a plastic bag. . . .
He held his muffler to his mouth and died—
No use. No use. It would not pass.

Anne

On the bed's edge,
everything rolled down now,
the heavy arms, shoulders, cooling—
her breast warm on her thigh,
the stretchmarks breathing. . . .
She was aware then, her knees opening, closing—
the chafings, the damp inner-folds, bruises—
their room dank with her smoking, locked;
four o'clock, the children sleeping. . . .
She was aware, toes clenched on the soiled garments,
the diaphragm pressing, rubbing,
was aware, a hand between her legs, holding, she
beyond his numb loneliness of words, there,
touching herself, musing, breathing her fingers, biting,
a girl-child trembling on a shoulder. . . .
And that evening, the dishes done,
wearing now a plain black dress,
there to the river's wide place
she came, where the ice was thin,
she, a country beauty,
and there went in.

The Moment of No Recovery

It's quiet there.
The clock can barely move
its holy arms.
The name of that gazing
virgin's face
is gone.
It was not clever,
nothing there
was clever.
Everywhere
but in her sly,
softening face
the good elation
is over.
It is not at all
symptomatic
that on this
tangible wall
in June she sees
one sailboat
on a lake of roses.
Sailboat, I think
I'm old enough
to be simple.
Great is the honoring

of Father and Mother.
I was drowning, I was
drowning, with my wings.

Chad Gadya, One Little Goat

O mister, I am your grandfather,
I sell my papers.
Don't beat me, don't take my money.
In my grave my eyes are open,
my shoes are high and broken,
my left arm ashes.
Filth, filth, is what I am.
I can't eat with these hands.
The lice soften my frozen clothing.
Life, life, your alley was sick
with rats and diphtheria.
Each day the men came home
with great bushels of bloody paper.
My daughters, we are starving here,
we are destroyed.
I hold both palms about your bellies—
If I let go! If I let go!
I had a dream
a street to play
everyone is wearing hats
and singing, singing in a circle,
"one little goat, one little goat."
The old mothers fill their windows laughing.

V

A Good Death

Father of Concord, the war comes!
Beautiful blue children call in the eastern field
bird songs? wave after wave? and forever?
If the world could be like him and sing,
if I could build my naked fear into that ecstasy
as Henry once could do and sigh,
or walk among the sad Waldens of the west
where love evolves that sweet face
called The Seasons. . . . All men must lie.
Like inborn gentleness they find
humiliation and then art.
A real life? A pond of simple reasons?
The smile changing to taste the dark?
The deep lake within the ordinary woman you lost?

If Henry sang like this to sing,
all rising from his loneliness to spring,
then no more excuses. The brave dream on.
The sleeping soldier smiles in the rain,
"a good death, a good death. . . ."
The world was born four billion years before.

Smiles of the Dreamer

That elm,
the cloud
that sweetens it,
the sky
looking after,
the wind
giving life
to all,
it is
a perfect
loving sight:
ages and ages.

Song

And so I stopped myself to play:
Black bells on the river,
Small candles on the barges far away—
These new women deep inside my mind
I had to have. Goodbye girls!
It's been a lovely time.
Morning would not have the world this way.
It's time to go. The sweet air makes me weep.
End high: "to hear, to touch, to kiss, to die,
With thee again in sweetest sympathy."

VI

Hospital Poem: May 22–24, 1970

I

Man beside me, Stanley,
soon to have an operation,
occluding artery in his head.
I think "serious," as if mine
were less serious:
thyroid tumor, *dangerous*.

May 22nd, Friday,
a windy warm day.
I'm young.
From my window bed
I can look out on trees
and uphill to the stars. . . .

A good room.
I can't concentrate
on the work I brought,
but I do read a little and talk,
feel sound but vulnerable to cheer.

Like flying: he might just die there
in the middle of a smile or when I wake up
changed and alive.
I'm forty. He is sixty-five.

If I die tomorrow
what do I write today,
what would I leave for them
in words to live on?

What is my truth?
I see them walking beyond
my life—as they will anyway—
my first son grown, his voice strange, the trouble
of his mind evolved to beauty and to strength
for that hard time of any human life.

People live on and leave the failed bodies behind.
The sun shines on fields of these old memories:
today the sun, tomorrow the sun,
the trees on the way, the iron fence
going uphill to school.

I've learned. Now learn more.

3

It will hurt and I will be afraid.
It will bleed and I will be
gray with drugs and conscious:
maybe it will be malignant. . . .
And I wonder at my mind.
What will I do in the dark,
the tubes in my nose and arm?
Oh well, I will come out like
that poor gray boy I saw
lying sideways on his heart.
It's funny. I'm laughing.
So serious and sad.

4

Sun, I'm happy to see you.
I'm a small child who has had pain and fear.
Now it's over for a while and I'm grateful
for your company.

Come up. Cover my day with your glory,
and I will play at immortality.

Hall of the Fifty Bells

Listening to time
in the hall
of the fifty
gilded bells.

Nothing has changed
since you looked away.

My face hides me
from your shy parents I see,

bundles on the steps
in the April
cold.

What is it? Who's there?

Intensive Care

1

This is the door where
Eva Turk bathed on the fourth floor.

I loved her. I was fourteen.
Her face is gone. That's all I remember.

2

Now I wait before Frankel's house,
my last best friend after the war.

As I doze against the wheel of my foreign car
the boys on the corner play stoopball

under the stop and one-way-arrow signs
at East 201st and Valentine.

Nineteen-forty-four.
It's all insane, the game.

3

Hi! I'm back in town again. How nice
to remember that old announcer's voice.

This Westinghouse kitchen radio that Paul heard
in the Kingsbridge Veterans' Hospital.

4

My work, she'll send it back.
I have no luck.

Working in the Fields of America

Last day of school. The sorrows
of leaving them and the good
work of the dead spring.

I'm sad. What will I do?
What will I do in the morning
now there will only be you?

I sit on the porch.
The summer is calm
and we are home.

Report cards!
No need to sign.
The radio's on
until September.

The Inertia

Then when they took me
from my first home, friend,
I carved into that windowsill
my mortal boyhood dates:
nineteen thirty, Born.
Died, nineteen forty.

And here is the same hand,
grown strong, then weak again,
a trembling thumb
that will not hold this paper,
a false hand stuffed
with the blood of sheep.

It's strange.
I want to weep
I run my hand along
this sloping attic wall.
Thirty years later, still,
I cover myself with my hand.

Candy

Everything in order
antiseptic, gay,
his body merely there,
no itching skin, no stain;
they change him every day.
The beds already made,
his tender shadow froze
at entrances of stone;
on benches never warm
he touched a childhood scar. . . .
O nothing, nothing's there—
it seized him where he was;
a veteran of grief
he shook and rising knew,
tore the neckband loose—
the others knew that face.
Frothing mouth and groin
he danced into the light:
The beach was all my own,
houses hammered shut—
drowsing, handsome, loved,
loving all there was;
it helped him from the wall.
Now everything is finished,
antiseptic, calm;

the family at his arm,
candy in his mouth,
he takes the sun.

Blue Roses

May I
wait
on your
stoop?

Mine is
never
in the sun-
shine.

        I'm not much
        to look
        at:

        Poems be
        my body of
        shining.

Respiratory: A Child's Poem

I woke today, phosphorescent; I was dying,
I was beginning to choke: I yawned, I shook,
oxygen gone, old fright forming
into my face.

Voice said, "You're a little boy. You have
a whole life to live. You're the greatest
young father poet in the whole world.
You're too young to be famous."

O thank you, spirit of air.
Your note was clear, signed by
beautiful Paula's golden pen.
Amen. I can breathe out again.

Boarding the Queen Anna Maria
Sept. 7th, 1971—12 Days to Haifa

Triglycerides, Uric Acid, Papillary Nodules:
as my skull grinds smaller with weather
I look up to myself appalled.

Thus I take my girl and frightened children,
kiss goodbye my mother and my father
and sail behind the world.

Meek man, tiny, solemn, violent man,
a teacher without a teacher,
a clerk without a star,
shove off! Your book
is finished.
Follow the autumn tide.

Kissing Goodbye

If I were younger
they would live longer.

If I stay
so do they.

(a tiny idea
going through my head
as I drive home)

Arthur's Moon

Now with his stiff back
and both shoulders
my father holds up
the binoculars.

A great night
on the terrace.

Boy, look at that moon!
Look at that moon!
It looks like it's right
on top of us.

VII

Songs for Paul Blackburn

I

The girl's dark face frowns,
"the ship is almost out of sight."
She bites her watch, chin on her
city-soft hands. "The water has calmed
down now." Yawns, smiles, embarrassed
she sees me, turns away.
"Look at the *boat,* Dad."
The milk-blue rock-flowers
of the cresting wake,
tiny blooms of glee.

2

The very small freighter moves low in the sea
beside our white ship, a froth of milk aft,
simple pale clouds motionless in the deep
planes above the bow. It is slower
with its weight of grain and single engine.
Slowly it falls behind us toward
the inexpressibly perfect sun: golden bridge,
red shining hull, and the tall blue stack.

I can look back on it now. Its captain
and crew are invisible and magical to me
as we sail closer to the sea
of the ancient Greeks. I will
still see its flag.

3

As I write quietly the men and women sleep
in bunks beside me. I stir. I press the pillows
deeply to uncover the fresh, wet faces
of my friends. They are all the way up here
drifting where I stand, their strange human
words tucked over them. Their life
is not sweet. I read for them.
We are all sailing too far.

4

The surface water moves with the wind,
changes from winter to spring,
knows the moon and sun,
knows living man and woman.

In the deep water there is
no star, no day.
It is night without end.
It is like the black of space
that is the natural light of our universe.

Untitled

I am swimming in salt water with my son.
Playing, I hold him up, save him, with my hand,
and say, "Imagine you are dreaming. You are
in a pool and you are beginning to drown.
Then suddenly a great hand grabs you and saves you.
You look around. It is your father."
He laughs and is very happy.

The girl in the ship's movie said
into the telephone,

"I'm feeling very
bad."

Selma's Story

The Melton Hat Company,
I worked as a trimmer.
Piecework, and for a fancy bow
with three folds you get 35 cents more.
To tell you the truth I was a slow worker.
I could make about four dozen, but some of
the girls could make six or seven.
The steam was so much
you couldn't even see the ceiling.
Then about ten years ago
the owner died and that
was the end of it.

After, we had our own place,
and I didn't have to wait
for the operator like in the factory.
I did my own operating.
My husband and I worked in the same factory,
but I didn't know him then.

Occupied Zone

The women walk along,
fish still jerking
in their netted sacks.
Their yellow bleeding eyes
glint at the flies.
As I pass by,
the new dust
of the fallen donkey
in my eye. . . .
We drive fast.
It is almost four
where Abraham endured
on the Hebron Road.
She says, "There may be war
before the end of the year."
I write, *The wet meats of the cactus
plunge up to speak!*
Lately, you've let your hair grow long
which makes me feel strong
and forlorn.

Fingertip

This tall thin nurse washing floors,
her orange gloves warm with rags,
sloshing the tile down, the dust.
Her three black plastic buckets.

These sparrowlike birds, fawny speckled,
delicate of beak, three splashing
in the humming drops of sun, smooth skulled
to the fingertip, like a bird's dream of birds.

Blue and Gray and Heather

The green curtains fall against the green wall.
Then this glass, the shiny knob and screen,
my clothes hanging: blue and gray and heather.
It is altogether unredeemed by my small breath
and by that artificial light so dim
over the orange tubes of the sink.

It's a bright cloudy day. I am high
and see the lavender desert far under the turning
tanks of clouds. Sparrows come to my ledge,
chilled and wet. If I could I would open
these window-doors and go out to them.

Coffee Room

Three gold stars on Carol's breasts.
My hands rest around my thumb I find.
You look great! Can I touch?
What happened, she smiles.
I know. You must be hornier today.
Your timing's great! Tomorrow
they're going to cut me open—
fingernail from naval to cunt.
I've been bleeding for seven months.
Well, I say, I want to see
the results for myself.
I hold her hand as long as I can.

Wind

A deep remarkable wind of the desert
slurring my brain.

Two o'clock heat.

Untired
my body falls asleep.

Inscription

Now Sonia dreams, tired of her heavy body
and the sun. She smiles and is young.
How cool here in this shade
under the ancient arch and pre-Christian wall.
The sand floor is fine in my hand.

I move to her bench recently placed for rest.
We look together through the sun-filled door and steps.
I follow up the stairwell, and she is wise.
Here we can see the whole Nabatean city
from its sunrise to its paradise.

"Lord, help your servant Nilus,
the builder of this place
and his children."
O good wife, it is a boulevard
we're walking down.

Something

Lashed by his son's insults
he thinks
as he tries to sleep
of the fence
in front of the swing
in the playground
where he was a boy—
Something
about the fence
as your feet
come up to it and then higher
something you felt
as you
let go of the chains.